FRAGILE FEELINGS

PART ONE - HURTING

Dedicated to all of the wounded souls trying to find their place in this wounded world.

♥

dear reader,

firstly, thank you for choosing my work to read.
secondly, i am so sorry if you can relate.

the themes in this book may stir up some painful memories and feelings you didn't realize you had buried inside of you.

please remember that it is okay to cry, it is okay to ask for help, it is okay to vent about something that happened a long time ago, it is okay to feel confused, it is okay to grieve, it is okay to feel angry, it is okay to feel nothing.

this book is here to make you feel seen and understood, not hurt you or judge you.

be gentle with yourself.

with love,

iris rose.

i am grieving people who are still alive.

family that betrayed me so badly,
i had no choice but to cut contact.
family that forced me to step on eggshells,
wounding my skin simply to keep the peace.

family stops becoming family,
the second they shatter your heart,
then abandon you without apology,
leaving you to pick up the pieces.

i kept searching for a home,
in other people, other places.

i was like playdough,
molding and morphing myself,
into shapes i thought were lovable.

that's what happens when you grow up
feeling like a constant burden.

you learn to disguise yourself as anyone else,
until you become a stranger to yourself.

i always feel like i'm in trouble,
like somebody is lurking around the corner,
watching my every move, ready to criticize.
paranoid that somebody is about to shout.

i always feel like i will to be blame,
i will be made to hang my head in shame.

even if i did nothing wrong,
even if it's not my fault,
i always become the scapegoat,
to someone else's misery.

i grieve who i could've been,
had i not lost years of my life,
to the mayhem in my mind.

a broken childhood is never buried;
it lives on in your mind, your heart, your soul.

the ruins will chase you around,
until you pay attention,
until you cry and grieve and rewire.

healing is a full time job,
with no wage.

i stopped expecting my parents to be parents
when i realized, they're wounded children,
trapped inside grown up bodies.

how can i expect them to take care of me,
when they can't even take care of themselves?

"why are you so anxious?"

the chaos of my childhood follows me about;
pulling on my sleeve,
afraid if i'm not hypervigilant,
one wrong move,
something is bound to catch me out.

that's how it was back then.
i had to slip about in silence,
monitoring everyone's emotions.
from the weight of every footstep,
to the sound of every sigh.

my anxiety is a blessing and a curse;
the anxiety that allowed me to survive,
stuck around in my body and mind,
making it so much harder to thrive.

my trauma did not make me stronger,
it made me fragile, sensitive, dysfunctional.

i struggle to trust good people.
i feel exhausted doing basic tasks.
i always feel behind, running on empty.
i became explosive, emotional, envious.

trauma does not strengthen people,
it shatters them completely.

i received praise for numbing out,
'you dealt with that well!'
'you're so resilient!'

on the inside i was screaming,
trying to claw my way out.

i received punishment for crying out,
'you're not dealing with this well!'
'you're falling apart!'
'don't be so dramatic!'

on the inside i was healing,
freeing my feelings.

sorry if the tears were inconvenient to you,
but your apathy was suffocating me.

the tears saved me,
the numbness almost killed me.

i've always been the therapist friend,
rushing to help heal broken hearts.

but when mine cracks into two
i cry alone under my covers,
holding it all in, hoping nobody hears.

i say 'mental health matters,'
then hate myself for the way i fall apart,
when i feel the slightest bit sad.

i say 'it's good to speak up,'
then stay completely silent.

i’m here but my body is always in that house.
i’m here, but i'm not really here.

my body has time traveled to the past.

i’m still seven years old,
wondering why they were born into
a home full of love and laughter,
and i was born into a house full of horrors.

'we had no idea, everything seemed fine.'

i was forced to smile, forced to mask the pain.
forced to stay loyal and protect a family
that was not loyal or protective of me.

everything seemed fine,
and that was part of the problem,
i wasn't allowed to have emotions.

i hope when we die,
our souls return to the stars.

so when we look up at night
nor you or i will ever be alone.

you're always shining down on me,
i'm always looking up at your light.

a shooting star is merely a soul,
taking the journey all the way back home.

having anxiety is like an endless earthquake,
shaking your insides, everyone running and
screaming, everything falling apart.

your body can't handle the havoc,
sweat, sickness, shakes, shivers.

yet you have to walk around straight-faced,
pretending you can't feel a natural disaster,
destroying everything inside of you.

be careful not to turn your healing
into self-harm in disguise.

the moment you judge yourself
for not feeling better already,
you've fallen into the vicious cycle.

you're not broken, you're wounded.
you're a person, not a project.
you need healing, not fixing.

i have no interest in revenge.
i don't want anyone to feel this pain.
i hope you heal so you stop hurting others.
i hope i heal so i don't end up being like you.

one parent was emotionally empty.
the other, emotionally explosive.

now i swing between

feeling nothing at all,
and feeling everything all at once.

my mother always needed mothering.

it becomes a bad habit, a self-sacrifice.

jumping and predicting everyone's every need,
feeling so much shame at the mere thought
of letting anyone down.

it becomes so futile, you lose any sense of self,
you forget you're also a human being,
with your own human needs.

dear inner child,

i'm so sorry you were the victim,
made to feel like the villain.

i'm so sorry you were expected to be calm,
in a whirlwind of chaos.

you were never asking for too much
to feel love, peace and safety.

you were never asking for too much
to live in a house that felt like home.

i cry on my birthday, christmas, new year.

i'm swallowed by the grief of time passing,
spat out by the grief of people from the past.

the more i pressure myself to appear happy,
the more hopeless and helpless i feel inside.

they tell victims
not to have a victim mindset.

they never tell predators
not to have a predator mindset.

nobody warns you how hard it is to heal,
to rewire your nervous system.

to not run or sabotage healthy love,
when all you've ever witnessed,
is dysfunctional dynamics.

it's like moving to another country;
the culture shock makes you homesick.

makes you want to run back home,
to all the places and people that hurt you,
to all you've ever known.

i try to act like
a capable and confident adult.

inside i'm still a little girl.

i'm still the little girl,
that sits shaking on the top of the stairs.

i'm still the little girl,
that needs to be comforted and held.

i'm still the little girl,
scared and confused by the world,
feeling completely abandoned and alone.

there is nothing more lonely,
than breaking generational trauma.

feeling all of the decades of pain,
generations have packed up and passed down,
knowing nobody else can feel it for you.

self-awareness first causes suffering,
then it eventually sets you free.

i feel like i'm too much, and not enough.
i feel like i'm too quiet, and too loud.
i feel like i'm too reserved, and too intense.

what i'm really saying is,
i feel like it's never safe to be who i truly am.

there is an empty pit swirling in my stomach
when i'm sat around the dinner table
with the people who've known me forever.

the truth is,
they've never really known me at all.

they never cared to ask, or to really listen.

we're all strangers, politely pretending
we know how to be a family to one another.

are you mad at me?
did i do something wrong?

your voice changed it's tone,
your energy was slightly off,
you're acting a little different.

you say it's nothing,
but i'm back in my childhood bedroom.

you say it's nothing,
but to me it feels like life or death.

i wish someone had told me,
there's not just a little kid inside of me,
but also a raging angry teen.

the little kid is frozen,
the teen is ready to fight.
together, they want to flee.

i want to hug my parents,
but it feels like holding onto a stranger.

stiff, awkward, unfamiliar.
like two puzzle pieces,
never meant to be side by side,
forced to fit together.

i don't feel held, i feel repulsed,
i feel the pain of the past in every embrace.
betrayal and unspoken stories,
a barrier of grief wedged between us.

deadbeat dad

my needs were ridiculously small,
you made them feel ridiculously large.

hold me, love me, protect me,
teach me basic things.

remember my birthday,
it's the same date every year.
you can even write it down,
set a reminder on your phone.
it would take just a minute,
to save me years of pain.

try not to prioritize a drink, a drug,
a meaningless love, before your child.

youtube has been more of a father to me
than you ever will be.

trauma is like being locked in a room,
lights turned off, tied to a chair.

forced to watch the worst parts
of your history's past,
over and over, day and night.

all while an audience chants,
'just get over it, just set yourself free!'
while they refuse to hand you the key.

violence is never a justifiable response
to the vulnerability of a child.

it shows strength to take responsibility
for your emotions and reactions.

it shows weakness to use an innocent being
as an emotional punching bag.

i was the golden child,
so mature for my age.

praised for parenting my parents,
when i should have been playing.

praised for perfect grades and good behavior,
when i should have been making mistakes.

praised for staying still and silent,
when i should have been speaking up.

my childhood was stolen from me,
now i feel a black hole in my chest,
sucking away any glimpse of light.

that's what you've been searching for,
that missing piece inside of you.

when i sleep at night, i don't get to rest.

i'm living in a second world,
i awaken into an inescapable hell.
trapped by my own subconscious mind,
night sweats and night terrors.

there's a gut-wrenching in-between
when you've gone no contact,
moved on from the past,
but not yet started your new life.

you feel empty and yet full of grief.

enough energy to let go, but not enough
to meet new people or find new passions.

you need deep rest and restoration,
but you're forced into solitude,
when you really want to be held.

when you find a home within yourself,
life feels a lot safer, a lot more stable.

you become less attached.

you know whatever happens,
you can always retreat back inside.
even if you forgot to visit for a little while,
you'll always be there waiting for you.

i was raised by the sound of slamming doors,
silent treatment and passive aggressive sighs.

silence is supposed to be peaceful,
but it meant something was seriously wrong.

like when birds stop singing, eerily quiet,
because danger is lurking around the corner.

i'm not sure if i'm more haunted
by everything i remember,
or by everything my brain has blanked out.

it's no surprise,
you have built walls around your heart.

you had to protect yourself,
from people who were meant to protect you.

what once helped you to survive,
is now making you suffer.

healthy love doesn't need
a defense mechanism.

when you are tempted to let in
a hot and cold type of love –

think of all of the sleepless nights,
the ones when you sobbed into your pillow,
feeling confused, feeling worthless,
wondering why you're not enough.

remember how exhausting it is to feel lifted up so
high, just to be dropped and dragged.

remember that you are not disposable,
you deserve consistency, you deserve stability.

remember that being alone is better than with
someone who makes you feel lonely.

you hurt my body,
but it was my brain you truly touched,
damaged with your deranged dirty hands.

the abuse is in the past,
but it lives on repeat in the present.

you get away without a scratch,
without a fragment of remorse and guilt.

i'm left to drown in a pool of shame,
for the pain you caused.

this depression is not something that disappears with a prescription drug or a run.

it's decades of disappointment,
stuffed deep down into my soul.

every layer i pull back,
reveals even more grief.

there is no overnight fix,
when digging up years of buried feelings.

‘its all in your head.’
yes, its all in my head,
that’s quite literally the problem.
in my head is my brain, a vital organ.

they call it a *mental* illness,
but a broken brain affects the entire body.

telling someone ‘it’s all in your head’ is as useless as telling someone having a heart attack that it’s ‘all in your heart.’

physically, i left that place.
mentally i'm still there.

the prison is my own mind,
i don't know how to escape it.

i never planned to live this long.
i was just trying to make it through each day.

i'm meeting myself for the first time,
figuring out who i am outside of the pain.

dreaming of death was escapism.

now i'm dreaming about a life,
i don't need to escape from.

i swing between empathy and anger.

empathy because i know they're in pain.

anger because i'm in pain too,
but i never use it as an excuse to hurt others.

i hate that phrase,
'everything happens for a reason.'

it's such a cruel thing to say to those
trampled by trauma or grieving
the loss of a loved one.

the wounded don't need lectures or lessons,
they need love, empathy and a helping hand.

i wear the weight of grief
like my favorite blanket.
afraid if i take it off,
i'll be exposed to the cold.

afraid if i take it off,
i'll forget the feeling of being
wrapped in your warmth.

i'm always longing to go home,
to a home i've never been before.
one where i feel safe,
a place i feel i truly belong.

i'm searching for that home,
inside my own mind and body.
it must be buried somewhere in there,
amongst all of that wreckage.

i finally walked away from the cycles
of devastation and drama.

now i feel lost somewhere;
in between the pain of the past,
and the peace i hope to find in the future.

addiction runs in my family.

instead of drink, drugs or drama,
i got addicted to self improvement.

self improvement becomes self harm
when you're running from yourself.

no amount of self help books
can feel your feelings for you.

no amount of productivity plans
can help you heal when you need
patience and understanding.

if you wouldn't say those harsh words to:

- your 5 year old self
- your best friend
- your loved one
- a stranger

you shouldn't be saying them to yourself,
you're worthy of the same love and respect.

i have such a hopeful heart,
for somebody with such a sad soul.

i've been through so much suffering,
and yet i still search for the good in the world.
i still hold onto hope for better days.

even when i'm at rock bottom,
i look up at the sun and know somehow,
the light will always return.

every older sibling deserves an older sibling.

instead, they become the person they needed
when they were younger.

they push people away,
act like they don't need anyone.
but behind closed doors,
they're still a little kid, scared of the world.

they can take care of themselves,
but they deserve to have someone
to protect and guide them too.

every older sibling deserves an older sibling.

your empathy helped you to escape,
to be duct tape in a broken home.

now your empathy is getting in the way,
of authentically being yourself.

you feel so much for everyone else,
you have no room left to feel
anything for yourself.

be an empathetic friend to yourself first,
the rest of the world can wait.

they say one day your story will be a survival guide to somebody else, and it's true.

but i hope one day you get to write a more beautiful story for yourself, one about the day you began to really live, not just survive.

you were labeled talented and gifted,
now facing shame and burnout,
for not achieving the same amount.

the people lying in hospital right now
aren't loved any less because they're
bedridden and unproductive.

this is evidence that your worth
is not about what you can do,
it's about who you are,
at your very core.

grief comes in unpredictable waves.

some are volatile, knocking you off of your feet,
submerging you in the storm.
others subtly ripple through your body.

grief comes in unpredictable waves,
but the tide is always in,
and there is no shore to rest upon.

no contact,
but i think of you every day.

no contact,
but i have so much left to say.

no contact,
but the memory of you is always in contact
with every fiber of my being.

it takes more than biological blood,
to create unbreakable bonds.

we don't share the same genes,
but we were born to be family.

we don't share the same history.
but together, we will create our own future.

one moment i care way too much,
the next i don't care about anything enough.

i'm exhausted from the back and forth,
doing everything i can to find a balance.

my childhood unfolded in extremes,
now i'm trapped in an all or nothing cycle.

we're the same age,
but i feel like i've fallen 10 years behind.

while you were finding passions,
i was figuring out how to stay alive.
while you were falling in love,
i was trying to escape a lack of love.

i spent the last decade in survival mode,
navigating a messy internal world,
so please be patient with me,
as i learn how to live for the very first time.

they say nobody is coming to save you,
but many people have saved me,
even if they didn't intend to.

it can be as small as a smile from a stranger,
a nudge from animal, words from a writer,
the lyrics to a song, an observant friend.

we are all saving each other every single day,
in tiny seemingly insignificant ways.

i try to hate the people that have hurt me,
but i only have a twisted kind of empathy.

i see their every trauma,
their every wound.

i psychoanalyze and know exactly
why they are the way they are.
their behavioral patterns are predictable.

i can't save them from themselves,
but i can save myself by seeing
it's nothing personal,
it's all a projection of pain.

hurt people hurt people,
healed people heal people.

i feel shame simmer through my body,
ordinary things feel morally wrong,
i feel watched, judged, out of place.

one wrong step
and i'll be screamed at.

one wrong step
and i'll be sent back to my bedroom.

one wrong step
and i'll be 5 years old, helpless again.

they ask me why i don't want to go out.

the smell of alcohol and cigarettes
is the scent of a party to them,
but the remnants of ruins to me.

it transports us both to another world;
them to one of spontaneity and escapism,
me to one of a traumatic childhood where
substances came before my wellbeing.

you're suspicious of kindness,
you were taught love is tied to tasks.
you were starving and given breadcrumbs,
expected to treat it like a banquet.

kindness does not ask you to treat yourself like a peasant, and the giver like royalty.

only narcissism and neglect does.

loneliness can be found in a crowd,
at a family dinner table,
in a picnic with friends,
in solitude during a sunset.

loneliness is not limited to age or being alone.

loneliness is about a lack of belonging,
a feeling of being unseen, and misunderstood,
a separation from feeling whole.

i'm not sure if i'm more afraid to exist in the world around me or the world inside of me.

they both feel completely out of my control.

the emptiness within me,
has led me on an endless pursuit.

i am always trying to fill that hole within me,
that heavy feeling in my chest.

i am always searching for something familiar,
yet completely unknown.

i don't have anything left to give
and yet here i find myself,
giving everything to everyone that asks,
abandoning myself to be of use to another.

i could give myself the world,
if i stopped giving it to everybody else.
the second i give myself a slither of attention,
i feel selfish and full of guilt.

it's a terrible pattern,
making myself uncomfortable,
to make others more comfortable.

i'm not at all motivated,
but there is this burning desire,
to make my inner child feel safe
and my future self feel proud.

he warned me,
'you'll never find anyone
that treats you better than i do.'

he would shatter my heart like glass,
then expect me to worship him
when he taped together a few shards.

telling me nobody else loves me enough
to risk cutting their skin on all this mess,
the mess he made, then blamed me for.

since leaving, i realized the truth,
nobody will ever treat me as badly as him.

i feel like a malfunctioning robot,
hardwired in all the wrong ways.

everyone seems to know what to do,
like it was programmed into them,
completely missed out of my machine.

i'm watching everyone,
mimicking what they do,
hoping nobody sees,
i'm falling behind, falling apart.

forever feeling
like a broken pile of scrap metal,
in a world full of flawless high tech.

when you are looking in the mirror,
picking every piece of yourself apart,
the little one living inside of you,
listening to every word you say.

tape a picture of yourself to the wall,
remember who you are talking to.

it's strange how you can share a childhood,
yet become strangers to your siblings.

they know everything about me,
yet simultaneously know nothing about me.

were we always just strangers,
surviving under the same roof?

i used to throw myself in the firing line
to protect my siblings from being a target.

i used to be a shield, a doormat,
a punching bag, a walking dear diary.

now i see why they use me like an object,
something they can pick up and put down
at their disposable.

sometimes they forget i'm human too.

help was such a foreign concept to me,
i used to apologize for bleeding on the bandages
they wrapped around my wounds.

when they tie their heart strings
around your lungs,
suffocating you,
so you cannot run away.

this is not love,
this is attachment.
this is fear of abandonment.

love doesn't hold you hostage,
love sets you free.

you say i'm *too* sensitive,
for falling apart whenever you shout.

i think you're fragile too,
and i feel so sorry for you.

you're frightened you will never be heard
unless you scream, shout and stomp about.

you act like a toddler throwing a tantrum,
because deep down you are.

you never healed that child within you,
the one nobody ever listened to.

you comfort yourself through repetition,
compensating for an unpredictable childhood.

the same shows, the same foods,
the same people, the same habits and routines.

there is no shame in seeking safety,
through the familiarity of the known,
when you have never had a comfort zone.

i used to avoid conflict to keep things calm,
not realizing silencing my own voice,
stirs up a raging war within.

there is no 'keeping the peace'
when you are sacrificing your own peace.

'don't argue back!'
they always used to say.

i wasn't trying to argue,
i was trying to explain my way.

now i turn silent in situations,
where i should voice my view.

i shut down at the slightest sign of conflict,
that's what i was always programmed to do.

i'm afraid to look into the mirror,
to see my mother's disappointed eyes,
staring right back at me.

'i'm trying my best,' she always used to say.
her best felt like the bare minimum,
i couldn't appreciate it at the time.
everything she was going through.

but i get it now,
i'm trying my best.

the worst part wasn't that you betrayed me,
i can live with not being able to trust you.
the worst part is questioning my own sanity.

i don't know how to trust myself,
after trusting you, again and again.

i don't know how to forgive myself,
after forgiving you, over and over.

it makes me sick to my stomach,
knowing you will never understand,
how badly you burned me.

my skin is still raw and tender,
yet you keep poking and prodding,
i'm screaming at you to stop.

but you can't hear me scream.
you could never hear me scream.
you silenced me before i ever could scream.

what were you wearing at the time?
why didn't you tell anyone?
why didn't you run away?

i was a child.
a few feet tall, with a manipulated mind.

he was a grown man.
6 feet tall, with a manipulative mind.

and you're telling me this is my fault?

all i want is a clear mind and untouched skin.

i never wanted to be strong and resilient.
i was a child, vulnerable to the world.
i wanted to be safe, protected and loved.

the more i fight depression,
the more it fights back.

it seems the only was to escape it,
is to completely detach.

the danger is, if you detach too much,
you begin to dissipate, dissociate, dissolve,
into the abyss of apathy.

so i'm left here under my covers,
i either cry it all out or stare at the wall,
wondering if life has any meaning at all.

i’m not an angry person,
but there is an angry person,
living inside of me,
completely rent free.

it’s not me,
it’s my father.

he paces around the
four corners of my mind,
searching for a reason
to release his rage.

i was an adult child,
a mother to my mother,
breaking myself apart,
to make her feel safe.

i was an adult child,
a father to my father,
shaking in my skin,
to soothe his rage.

now i need to be both;
a mother and a father,
to the wounded child,
trapped inside this adult body.

dear dad,

i've given up hope
that you'll be the father i need.

i'm not angry anymore, but you should know,
you've disappointed the little girl
that lives inside of me.

the saddest thing of all is she would've forgiven you
one hundred times over if you had asked her to.

but me? i'll never forgive you for hurting her.

she never asked for anything but love.
you couldn't even provide the one thing that is
supposed to be given so naturally.

do you know what that does to the psyche?

they say it gets better,
but every time it gets better,
i realize how much i've missed out on,
and i begin to feel so much worse.

i grieve the years i've lost to grief.

i was daddy's little girl,
for a brief moment in time.

then i grew up,
started being my own person,
and now i'm a stranger to my father.

but deep inside me,
that little girl still lives,
still believing she is daddy's whole world,
when she isn't even on daddy's mind.

i never needed you to be perfect,
i never expected you to be flawless.

i just needed you to take responsibility,
acknowledge and apologize,
when you messed up.

the bar was already so low,
and you still kicked it to the floor.

i'm haunted by who i could've been...
if i had the energy levels of a normal person.
if i had grown up in a stable loving home.
if i had left that relationship sooner.

i know it's pointless to dwell on the past,
but the lost potential still haunts my present.

my therapist told me i'm really self-aware,
but i just need someone to recognize,
that's literally the problem.

i can't go a single second without psychoanalyzing
and intellectualizing
my every thought and feeling.

being so aware is eating me alive,
i never get any mental rest.

'just wait until you have kids!'
they used to always say,
to justify the pain.

now i look at children,
and i'm even more confused.

how can you be so cruel and relentless,
to somebody so small and innocent.

if i could go back in time,
i'd just let my younger self know,
it's not their fault and promise them,
we eventually make it out of that hell.

i'm constantly reminding myself,
i am safe now.

but i never truly feel safe,
i'm always on high alert.
feeling frozen and empty,
or restless and anxious.

i've forgotten how it feels,
to just feel normal.

i've always had so much love to give,
i've always given it to the wrong people.
pouring and pouring into problems,
until there was nothing left to give.

i always feel like i'm falling behind,
always out of breath, attempting to catch up.

i spent my whole childhood being told,
i'm very mature for my age.

now i feel stunted in every possible way.

when you've been starving,
you learn to eat anything edible.

now imagine what happens,
when you are withheld love.

we take whatever we're given,
even when we know we deserve better.

it feels like we have to, simply to survive.

the most disheartening part is when you try to do *everything* to heal, and still feel exactly the same as before; broken and hard to love.

my trauma is complex.

i don't remember everything that happened.
i don't know exactly what triggered me.
i don't know how to trust others.
i don't know what i need.

my trauma is complex.

it makes me feel like i'm too complex,
to ever truly be loved.

when one parent would run away,
and one would never leave you alone,
you end up in a push-pull relationship
with yourself.

one minute,
running away from yourself.

the next minute,
judging every little thing you do.

i feel everything so deeply.

i don't know how to be any other way,
my logical mind is too illogical to use,
i have to feel my way through the world.

i've been heartbroken before,
but i question if i've ever really known love.

maybe it was all some weird attachment.
maybe the heartbreak wasn't about losing love,
but about the feeling of abandonment.

love is supposed to be calm and consistent,
all i've ever felt is chaos and fear.

they say what doesn't kill you
makes you stronger.

what didn't kill me,
has made me hypersensitive.

what didn't kill me,
has created mayhem in my mind.

what didn't kill me,
has made it impossible to feel alive.

i envy those who can run to their parents
whenever they're in trouble.

knowing they can fall backwards,
land softly and have love guide the way.

i run from mine when i have a problem,
knowing i'll get into more trouble,
for getting myself into trouble.

when you lose somebody,
your entire world is flipped upside down.

yet the entire world keeps turning,
as if nothing has changed,
as if everything is exactly as it's meant to be.

you feel homesick for a home,
you can no longer visit.

when you never fit into your family,
you can carry this deep rooted belief,
that you'll never really belong anywhere.

it makes you run and hide,
it makes you stay inside
when really, you want nothing more,
than to finally feel seen.

that's a dangerously lonely way to live.

love to me is like going to a new country.

everyone is speaking the same language,
it's all around me, i know it exists,
but i have no idea what anyone is saying.

i need the kind of rest sleep can never bring.

to completely pause time and lie in the grass,
as earth wraps herself around me and says,
'take as long as you need.'

i have an ambitious heart,
and a body riddled with anxiety.

it seems nothing i ever do,
is good enough for me.

i tell myself i'll feel proud,
once i scale the next mountain.

but i never do, at most,
only a temporary sigh of relief.

i became addicted to breadcrumbs.

checking and waiting,
like my life depended on it.
feeling like if i wasn't fed, i would drop dead.

it was pathetic,
but at least it occupied my mind.
something i was desperate to escape from.

i'm anticipating the heartbreak.

the heartbreak of trying to explain,
it's not their fault that you're never around.

the heartbreak of trying to explain,
nothing they do can mend the past.

the heartbreak of trying to keep it all together,
when the thought of you makes me fall apart.

i long for the day i wake up
without being weighed down
by the heaviness of my heart.

that constant dull ache,
robbing me of anything light.

my broken childhood has taught me,
i'd rather spend all of my time alone,
than be where i don't feel like i belong.

the loneliness of feeling out of place,
is far worse than the loneliness of being alone.

it’s emotionally exhausting,
being so self aware,
yet so mentally unwell.

i’m a witness to my own crimes.

i'm trying so desperately to heal.

but nothing shakes the feeling,
that i'm completely broken inside,
that no amount of healing can return,
the childhood that was stolen from me.

you know deep down,
they're never going to change.
it's not your job to fix them,
and fixing them will not fix your pain.

you know deep down,
you deserve better.

be honest with yourself.

i long for a love
that makes me feel understood.

a love that sees everything,
the best of me, the worst of me,
and still chooses to stay anyway.

not because they feel they have to,
but because they really want to.

at the same time,
i'm deeply afraid of this love.
it's such a foreign concept to me.

some people don't understand,
how much energy it takes,
just to feel perpetually unsafe.

it doesn't matter what you have in life,
if you don't feel safe in your own body,
you spend every day in complete misery.

therapy is helping,
but sometimes i need,
real human intimacy.

not somebody paid to listen.

i need somebody to hold my hand,
without any ulterior motive.

to silently say,
'i'm here, i'm here to stay.'

i don't know how to be a functioning member of
society when my insides are completely dysfunctional.

i don't know how to be human when i feel like a
monster has taken over my mind.

i don't know how to go on when my body is so
heavy it feels like i'm destined to fall.

the most devastating part is when
you open your heart to trust new people,
just to be let down in the exact same way.

or even worse,
you let yourself down in the exact same way.

you can spend so much time mending your heart just
for it to be instantly bent, squeezed and twisted out of
shape.

if i was my father's father,
i'd teach him not to be so afraid of his feelings.
i'd teach him that it takes strength to be soft,
i'd teach him there is no life without love.

i tried teaching him,
as his daughter,
but he won't listen.

he still sees me as a little girl,
with nothing useful to say,
a little girl, standing in his way.

my brother was my first bully.

nitpicking at every little thing,
putting me in physical
and psychological pain,
every damn day.

'typical sibling rivalry,' they used to say.
but if he wasn't my sibling,
and had treated me that way,
i would've been protected.

he would've been taken away.

the sick unspoken rule.

we share the same DNA,
that doesn't entitle you,
to treat me in any particular way.

you birthed a human,
not a maid, not a therapist, not a slave.

for me, the emotional abuse
was worse than anything physical.

when they mess with your mind,
it makes you feel like you're going crazy.
it makes you feel like you're beyond fixable.

my skin is resilient,
but my mind is not.

at least when it is physical,
it can be seen, it can be validated.

when it's emotional, mental,
it can only be felt, it's an invisible pain.

my triggers are unpredictable.

an innocent hand touches my arm.
it's a thursday, in april.
his eyes have the same glare.
the air has that scent to it.

it's an exhausting way to live,
not knowing what will throw you
back into the trauma of the past.

in dangerous situations,
i feel completely calm,
i feel resilient and prepared,
i can take the lead, figure it out.

but in everyday life, i feel useless.
i feel anxious over mundane things,
i feel completely lost with what to do,
how to be, who to be, what to say.

quieten down, speak up.
stay out of the way, do more to help.
you're expensive, you're a burden.
figure it out yourself, you're doing it wrong.
don't ask for anything, why didn't you ask?
don't bother me, the phone goes both ways.

mixed messages my entire childhood,
now i get high on hot and cold behavior.

it's a blessing and a curse,
the empathy my twisted past gave me.

i can make other people feel seen,
but i also carry other people's pain,
as if i'm the one to blame.

i spend so much time absorbing
everyone's feelings,
i can no longer recognize my own.

i wasn't just lying to my loved ones
about who you are, i was lying to myself.

not because of what you did to me,
but because it meant facing myself.

facing the part of me that must've felt so worthless,
so unlovable, that she would stay in places that ripped
her apart, limb by limb.

i feel sad about the fact i feel sad,
i feel angry that i feel angry,
i feel ashamed of my shame,
i feel grief for all of the grief i feel.

it's not as simple as letting my emotions go,
there are so many layers to everything i feel.

i'm tired of being told to step out of my comfort zone,
when i've never had a comfort zone to step out of.

i'm tired of being told i need to fix everything,
when i never broke anything in the first place.

Made in the USA
Columbia, SC
24 August 2024

41089426R00078